This book belongs to:

25696899R00062

Made in the USA
San Bernardino, CA
12 February 2019